PLAY BALL!

written by Glen Harlan
illustrated by Richard Hull

HARCOURT BRACE & COMPANY

Orlando Atlanta Austin Boston San Francisco Chicago Dallas New York
Toronto London

Who will pitch here?
Dog will pitch!

Who will catch here?
Horse will catch!

Who will stand here?
Bear will stand!

Who will throw here?
Cat will throw!

Who will chase here?
Sheep will chase!

Who will stop here?
Pig will stop!

Who will play here?
Everyone will play!